Sound Advice on

Developing Your Home Studio

by Bill Gibson

ProAudio
press

236 Georgia Street, Suite 100
Vallejo, CA 94590
(707) 554-1935

©2002 Bill Gibson

Publisher: Mike Lawson
Art Director: Stephen Ramirez; Editor: Patrick Runkle

Cover image courtesy Midas.

ProAudio Press is an imprint of artistpro.com, LLC
236 Georgia Street, Suite 100
Vallejo, CA 94590
(707) 554-1935

Also from ProMusic Press
Music Copyright for the New Millennium
The Mellotron Book
Electronic Music Pioneers

Also from EMBooks
The Independent Working Musician
Making the Ultimate Demo, 2nd Ed.
Remix: The Electronic Music Explosion
Making Music with Your Computer, 2nd Ed.
Anatomy of a Home Studio
The EM Guide to the Roland VS-880

Also from MixBooks
The AudioPro Home Recording Course, Volumes I, II, and III
The Art of Mixing: A Visual Guide to Recording, Engineering, and Production
The Mixing Engineer's Handbook
The Mastering Engineer's Handbook
Music Publishing: The Real Road to Music Business Success, Rev. and Exp. 5th Ed.
How to Run a Recording Session
The Professional Musician's Internet Guide
The Songwriters Guide to Collaboration, Rev. and Exp. 2nd Ed.
Critical Listening and Auditory Perception
Modular Digital Multitracks: The Power User's Guide, Rev. Ed.
Professional Microphone Techniques
Sound for Picture, 2nd Ed.
Music Producers, 2nd Ed.
Live Sound Reinforcement
Professional Sound Reinforcement Techniques
Creative Music Production: Joe Meek's Bold Techniques

Printed in Auburn Hills, MI
ISBN 1-931140-26-X

Contents

Setting Up Your Studio

Each home studio has a unique personality depending on several factors. If money is no issue then your home studio can function in much the same way as the most sophisticated studio in the world. However, the vast majority of home recording setups are built on a shoestring budget where creativity in the use of available gear is much more powerful than the actual equipment.

This book will help you get the most out of the gear you have. We'll look at basic operational procedures, inter-connectivity, monitoring and cabling considerations, some technical jargon, and some acoustical considerations. We'll also jump into different theories of mixing, how to set up a mix, mastering and other musical considerations.

Professional Amplifiers

Connecting the mixer to your power amp is an important step. Use quality line cables (like the type you use for a guitar or keyboard) to connect the output of the mixer to the input of the power amp. Many wires are specially designed for minimal signal loss. This means a better signal-to-noise ratio. Quality wires and connectors also last longer and create fewer problems.

Using a quality power amp is very important. Distortion is a primary cause of ear fatigue, and an amplifier that produces less distortion over longer periods of time causes less fatigue and damage to your ears.

If you have a professional power amp with a rating of at least 100 watts RMS and if you use a good quality reference monitor designed for studio use, you'll be able to work on your music longer with less ear fatigue. When I use the term professional in regard to amplifiers, I mean an industrial strength unit, designed for constant use in a pro setting. Compared to a consumer home amplifier, amps designed for pro use generally have better specifications, therefore helping to reduce ear fatigue. They use high quality components, which last longer and work harder for longer periods of time. Reputable manufacturers offer the best service and support. Fast, quality service is invaluable when you're making money with your equipment.

Cabling Considerations

Proper Speaker Wire

Use the proper wire to connect your speakers to your power amp. Speaker wire is not the same as a guitar cable. Use designated speaker wire. Guitar cable is designed to carry signals like those from a keyboard to a mixer, not power from an amplifier to speakers. Also, choosing wire that's too thick or too thin for your situation can cause a problem with the efficiency of your amp and speakers.

Ask a salesperson which wire gauge and type is best for your situation. Let them know how long a run it is from your power amp to your speakers, what kind of connectors your amp has, plus the brand of your amp and its power rating. If the salesperson gives you a glazed look when you recite all of these specifications, this indicates that they don't understand your situation. I suggest you get a second opinion.

As a rule of thumb, a good quality 18-gauge speaker wire works well in most cases.

Some Cable Theory
A cable recognizes a signal as voltage (electrical current). Small voltages travel down interconnecting cables (line level, instrument, data) and relatively large voltages (currents) travel down speaker

cables. A magnetic field is created in and around a conductor as it passes electrical current. Any materials that optimize the accuracy of this conductance help the accuracy of the transfer process. Any design that takes into consideration the full-bandwidth of audio signal relative to frequency, time, and content becomes

Speaker Wire Gauge

Always use heavy-duty wire designed specifically for use with speakers. The chart below indicates suggested wire gauges for varying lengths. The smaller the wire number, the thicker the wire. Thicker wire has less resistance to signal. To have minimal degradation of signal in longer runs, we use thicker wire.

Be absolutely certain that the red post on the back of the power amp is connected to the red post on the back of both speakers and that black goes to black!

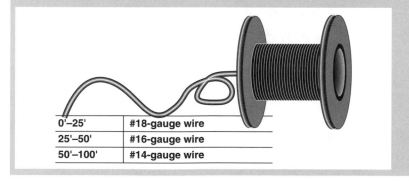

0'–25'	#18-gauge wire
25'–50'	#16-gauge wire
50'–100'	#14-gauge wire

complex—more complex than simply connecting a copper wire between the output and input.

Once a few manufacturers addressed the effect of cable on sound, it became apparent to those who truly cared about the quality of their audio work that cable design makes a difference. Most inexpensive cables consist of a conductor that's made of copper strands and a braided shield to help diffuse interference. Not much consideration is given to bandwidth relative to frequency-specific capacitance, and potential frequency-specific delay considerations.

Two main considerations must be addressed in cable design: balance of amplitude across the full audio bandwidth and the time delays as different frequencies transmit throughout the cable length.

1. Balance of Amplitude—Monster Cable addresses this with their Amplitude

Balanced®Multiple Gauged Conductors. Since there are different depths of penetration into the conductor material by various frequency ranges, certain conductor sizes more accurately transmit specific frequencies. Therefore, it's implied that optimal conductance is accomplished by conductors that match the bandwidth penetration depth. With the frequency range divided among multiple types and sizes of wire, each frequency is carried in an optimized way.

2. Timing Considerations—High frequencies travel at a higher rate than low frequencies throughout the length of a conductor (wire). Low frequencies can't be sped up, but high frequencies can be slowed down by winding the high-frequency conductors to create inductance at those frequencies. When the windings cause the correct inductance at the specified frequency bands, all frequencies arrive at their destination in accurate and precise timing and

phase relation. This corrected phase relationship restores the soundstage dimensionality, imaging, and depth. When the frequencies arrive out-of-phase, they exhibit time-domain distortions of phase coherence and transient clarity.

Do Cables Really Sound Different?

The difference between the sound of a poorly designed and a brilliantly designed cable is extreme in most cases. If a narrow bandwidth signal comprised of mid frequencies and few transients is compared on two vastly different cables, the audible differences might be minimal. However, when full-bandwidth audio, rich in transient content, dimensionality, and depth, is compared between a marginal and an excellent cable, there will typically be a dramatic and noticeable difference in sound quality.

If your microphone cables are of inferior quality, anything you record through

Sound Advice on Developing Your Home Studio

them will be less full and contain less transient accuracy than if you used excellent mic cables. The same concerns apply to instrument cables, patch cables, and digital interconnect cables.

Listen to Audio Example 1. The acoustic guitar is first miked and recorded through some common quality cable. Then it's recorded through a microphone with some very high quality Monster Studio Pro 1000 Cable. Notice the difference in transient sounds, depth, and transparency.

Audio Example 1
Common Mic Cable then Monster Cable

Audio Example 2 demonstrates the difference in vocal sound using marginal mic cable first, then a high-quality Monster Cable. Notice the difference in transient sounds, depth, and transparency.

Audio Example 2
Common Cable then Monster Cable

The following Audio Example is difficult to quantify because it involves my subjective opinion. However, I include it because I've experienced an extreme quality difference at this particular point in the signal path when cable changes were made. The comparisons in the previous two audio examples were performed with only one change in each example: the cable. In this example, I'll record an acoustic guitar while monitoring through powered monitors that are first connected to my mixer with inferior cables and then connected with superior cables. My effort is focused on making the two examples sound the same when I monitor them. My EQ decisions are made based on the sound I hear. Listen to see if you can tell a difference between the guitar sounds in Audio Example 3.

Audio Example 3

Monitor Cable Comparison

Digital interconnect cables also have an effect on the sound quality of digital masters and clones. Test this theory out on your system. Start integrating high quality cables where they'll make a big difference and where you can change the least amount of cable to achieve cable integrity without a weak link.

Studio Monitors

Selecting speakers is the key to producing good sounds that reliably transfer from your system to a friend's system or your car stereo. One of the most annoying and frustrating audio recording problems is a mix that sounds great on your system but sounds terrible everywhere else.

Part of the solution to this is experience with analytical listening on your system to music that you know sounds good everywhere. Possibly, an even bigger part of the solution to this problem lies in the use of near-field reference monitors.

Industry standards are continually changing and the market for near-field reference monitors has become very competitive. There are great new products available from all major speaker manufacturers, and most are very reasonably priced (typically between $300 and $1000 per pair).

Several manufacturers are producing high priced near-field reference monitors—some with built-in, factory-calibrated amplifiers. Often these speaker pairs cost several thousand dollars and are very accurate and quite fun to listen to, but they aren't necessary for most home studio applications.

Near-Field Reference Monitors

A near-field reference monitor is designed to be listened to with your head at one point of an equilateral triangle (approximately three feet, or one meter, on each side) and the speakers at the other two points. The speakers should be facing directly at your ears and are ideally

Sound Advice on Developing Your Home Studio

about 10 degrees above the horizontal plane that's even with your ears. With this kind of a system, the room that you're monitoring in has a minimal effect on how you hear the mix. These monitors should sound pretty much the same in your studio at home as they do in any studio in the world.

If the room is minimally affecting what you hear, then the mix that you create will be more accurate and will sound good on more systems. Changing to a near field reference monitor gives you immediate gratification through more reliable mixes, plus it lets you start gaining experience based on a predictable and accurate listening environment.

Not just any small speaker works as a near-field reference monitor. In fact, speakers that aren't designed specifically for this application produce poor results and unreliable mixes when positioned as near-field reference monitors.

Near-Field Reference Monitors

Your head should be at one point of a one-meter triangle and the monitors should be at the other, parallel to and aimed at your ears or 10 degrees down at your ears.

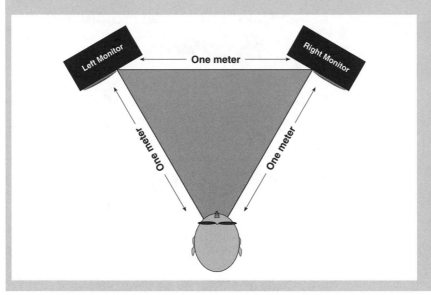

Far-Field Monitors

Far-field monitors are designed to be farther away from the mixing engineer, and their sound is greatly affected by the acoustics of the room they're in. Larger rooms have more air to move, so they

Sound Advice on Developing Your Home Studio

require larger monitors to move that air. These monitors can be very expensive.

In order to get great results from far-field monitors, they must be used in a studio that has been acoustically designed for a smooth and even balance of frequencies within the room. Since this can involve actual construction and often plenty of expense and since near-field reference monitors can produce excellent results, the obvious choice for most home setups is a pair of near field reference monitors.

Connectors

We encounter several types of connectors when hooking audio equipment together. In this section, we cover RCA connectors, 1/4-inch connectors, XLR connectors, adapters, plugging in, powering up/down, grounding and hums.

RCA Connectors

RCA phono connectors are the type found on most home stereo equipment and are physically smaller in size than the plug that goes into a guitar or keyboard. RCA phono connectors are very common in home-recording equipment and are among the least expensive connectors.

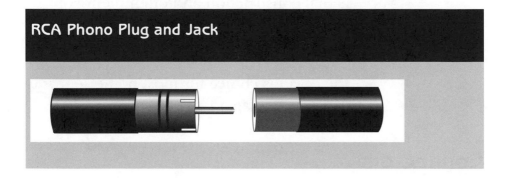

RCA Phono Plug and Jack

Quarter-inch Phone Connectors

Quarter-inch phone connectors are the type found on regular cables for guitars or keyboards. These connectors are commonly used on musical instruments and in home and professional recording studios.

Notice that a guitar cable has one tip and one sleeve on the connector. In a guitar cable, the wire connected to the tip carries the actual musical signal. The wire carrying the signal is called the hot wire or hot lead. The sleeve is connected to the braided shield that's around the hot wire. The purpose of the shield is to diffuse outside interference, like electrostatic interference and extraneous radio signals.

The other type of 1/4-inch phone connector is the type found on stereo headphones. This plug has one tip, one small ring (next to the tip) and a sleeve. In headphones, the tip and ring are for the left and right musical signal, and the sleeve is connected to the braided shield that surrounds the two hot wires. This connector can be used for other devices that require a three-point connection.

XLR Connectors

XLR connectors are the type found on most microphones and the mic inputs of most mixers. Two of the three pins on this connector carry the signal, and the third is connected to the shield. The reason for the two hot leads has to do with reducing noise in a balanced low-impedance mic cable. The details involved here are covered later in this book.

1/4" Phone Plug (Mono)

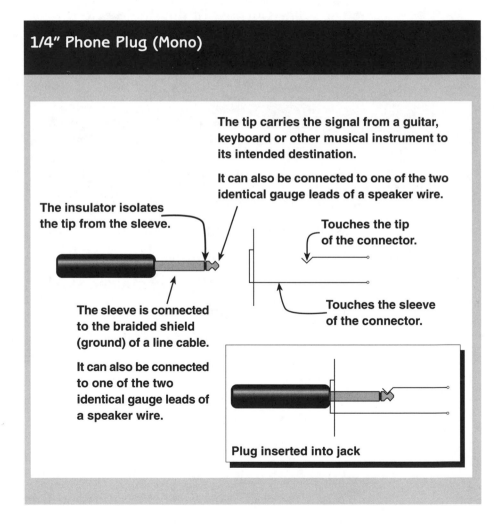

The tip carries the signal from a guitar, keyboard or other musical instrument to its intended destination.

It can also be connected to one of the two identical gauge leads of a speaker wire.

The insulator isolates the tip from the sleeve.

Touches the tip of the connector.

The sleeve is connected to the braided shield (ground) of a line cable.

It can also be connected to one of the two identical gauge leads of a speaker wire.

Touches the sleeve of the connector.

Plug inserted into jack

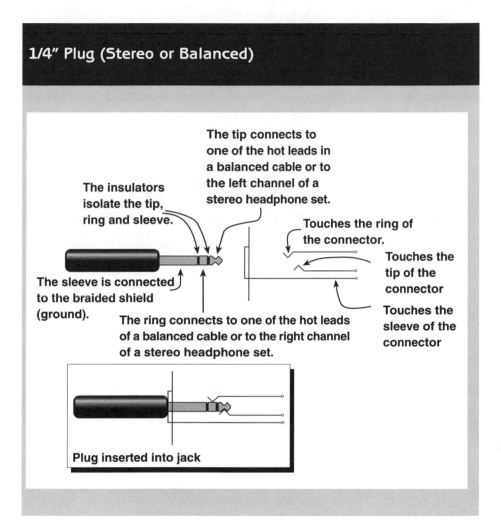

The tip connects to one of the hot leads in a balanced cable or to the left channel of a stereo headphone set.

The insulators isolate the tip, ring and sleeve.

Touches the ring of the connector.

Touches the tip of the connector

The sleeve is connected to the braided shield (ground).

The ring connects to one of the hot leads of a balanced cable or to the right channel of a stereo headphone set.

Touches the sleeve of the connector

Plug inserted into jack

It's not uncommon to find cables with an XLR on one end and a 1/4-inch phone plug on the other or cables that have been intentionally wired in a nonstandard way. These are usually for specific applications and can be useful in certain situations. Check wiring details in your equipment manuals to see if these will work for you.

There are other types of connectors, but RCA phono, 1/4-inch phone and XLR are the most common. It's okay to use adapters to go from one type of connector to another, but always be sure to use connectors and adapters with the same number of points. For example, if a plug has a tip, ring and sleeve, it must be plugged into a jack that accepts all three points.

The XLR Connector

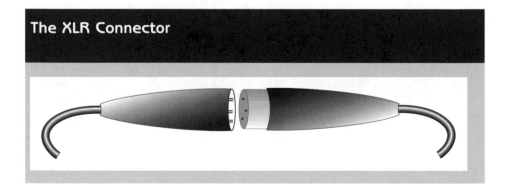

- *The center post on the RCA phono plug corresponds to the tip on the RCA-to-1/4" phone plug adapter.*

- *The tip and the ring on the 1/4" tip-ring-sleeve phone plug correspond to pins 2 and 3 on the 1/4" phone plug-to-XLR adapter. The sleeve corresponds to pin 1. The pin numbers of the XLR connector are imprinted on the connector end itself. They're located next to the base of the pins on the male XLR connector and next to the holes on the female XLR connector.*

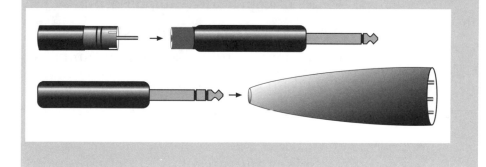

Plugging In

The output of your mixer might have multiple outputs for connection to different amplifier inputs. The stereo line output is the correct output from the mixer to be plugged into the power amplifier. This might also be labeled Main Output, Mains, Mix Out, Control Room Monitor Output, Out to Amp, or Stereo Out. If your mixer has XLR outputs available and if your power amp has XLR inputs, patch these points together as your first choice. This output typically provides the most clean and noise-free signal.

Electrical Power

When plugging into the power outlet, use power strips that have protection against power surges and spikes. These can be picked up for a reasonable price at most electrical supply stores.

Spikes and surges are fluctuations in your electrical current that rise well above the 120-volt current that runs most of your equipment. Surges generally last longer than spikes, but both usually occur so quickly that you don't even notice them. Since power surges and spikes can seriously damage delicate electronic circuits, protection is necessary for any microprocessor-controlled equipment (computers, synthesizers, mixers, processors, sequencers, printers, etc.).

Powering up
- Turn on the mixer and outboard gear (like delays, reverbs and compressors) before the power amps.

- Always turn power amps on last to protect speakers from pops and blasts as the rest of the electronic gear comes on.

Powering down
- Turn power amps off first to protect speakers, then turn the mixer and outboard gear off.

Grounding

Grounding is a very important consideration in any recording setup. The purpose of grounding is safety. If there's an electrical short, or a problem in a circuit, the electricity may search out a path other than the one intended. Electricity is always attracted to something connected to the ground we walk on (the earth). The reason for the third pin, called the ground pin, on your AC power cable is to give an electrical problem like this some-where to go other than through you.

The ground pin in your electrical wiring is ideally connected through the third pin on your power cord to a grounding rod, which is a metal rod that's stuck at least six feet into the earth. Another possible source of ground is a metal pipe like the water supply pipe to your hot-water heater. This can be an excellent ground, but be sure the metal pipe at the heater is not connected to plastic pipe before it gets to ground.

If you happen to touch equipment that isn't properly grounded and if you are standing on the ground, you become just the path to the ground that the electricity is looking for. This could, at the very least, be painful or, at worst, even fatal. Properly grounding a piece of equipment gives potentially damaging electrical problems a path, other than you, to ground.

AC Plug into Ground Lifter

A problem can occur when different pieces of equipment are connected to different outlets. An inconsistency in ground and in-house wiring can produce a low hum in your audio signal. When this happens, you can use a ground lifter on the piece of equipment causing the hum. If you have consistent ground problems consult an electrical engineer. It'll save you time and pain.

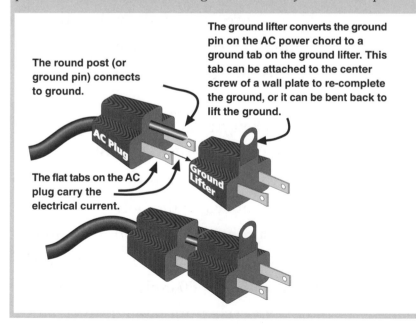

The ground lifter converts the ground pin on the AC power chord to a ground tab on the ground lifter. This tab can be attached to the center screw of a wall plate to re-complete the ground, or it can be bent back to lift the ground.

The round post (or ground pin) connects to ground.

The flat tabs on the AC plug carry the electrical current.

Ground Hum

Aside from causing physical pain, grounding problems can induce an irritating hum into your audio signal. If you have ever had this kind of noise show up mysteriously and at the worst times in your recordings, you know true frustration.

Audio Example 4
60-Cycle Hum

Sixty-cycle hum is the result of a grounding problem where the 60-cycle electrical current from the wall outlet is inducing a 60-cycle-per-second tone into your musical signal.

To make matters worse, this 60-cycle tone isn't just a pure and simple 60 Hertz sine wave. A sine wave is the simplest wave form and, in fact, is the only wave form that has a completely smooth crest and trough as it completes its cycle. We could easily eliminate a 60-cycle sine wave with a filter. Sixty-cycle hum has a distinct and distracting wave form, which also includes various harmonics that extend into the upper frequencies.

It's very important to have your setup properly grounded in order to eliminate 60-cycle hum and for your own physical safety while operating your equipment.

The Sine Wave

There are 360° in the complete cycle of a sine wave. This is the simplest wave form, having a smooth crest and trough plus complete symmetry between positive and negative air pressure.

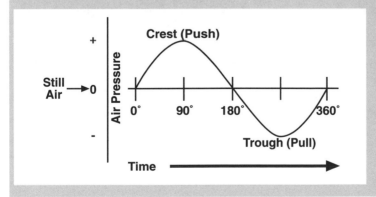

Grounding Tips

The best approach to a persistent grounding problem is to hire a qualified electrician to rewire your studio so that all available electrical outlets have the ground terminals running to the exact same perfect ground.

Lifting the ground doesn't necessarily mean nothing is grounded; it simply means that a particular piece of equipment isn't grounded twice to conflicting grounds. Many home studios have the ground lifted on all pieces of gear except one.

Another way to eliminate hum is to disconnect the shield at one end of your line cable (patch cable, instrument cable, guitar cord, etc.), usually at the end closest to your mixer. This can break the ground loop and solve the problem.

Danger! Remember, the human body can conduct the flow of 20 to 30 amps of 110-volt alternating current (AC). Since this can be, at the very least, very painful or, at worst, even lethal, be cautious.

Sound Advice on Developing Your Home Studio

Importance of the Mixer

Audio Examples 5, 6 and 7 are mixed in three different ways—same music and board but different mixes. Notice the dramatic differences in the effect and feeling of these mixes. Even though they all contain the same instrumentation and orchestration, the mixer combined the available textures differently in each example.

Audio Examples 5, 6 and 7
Mixes 1, 2 and 3

We can control a number of variables at a number of points in the pathway from the sound source to the recorder and back. This pathway is called the signal path. Each point holds its own possibility for degrading or enhancing the audio integrity of your music. When setting up your studio it is of paramount importance that you fully understand and implement proper interconnection procedures.

Matching Inputs/Impedance

Impedance is, by definition, the resistance to the flow of current measured in a unit called an ohm. Imagine two pipes: one large and one small. More water can go through the large pipe with less resistance than the same amount of water through the small pipe. I think we would all agree that a city water reservoir would be easier to drain through a six-foot diameter pipe than through a straw. The large pipe represents low-impedance (low resistance). The small pipe represents high-impedance (high resistance).

We can put a numerical tag on impedance. High impedance has high resistance, in the range of 10,000 to 20,000 ohms (a small pipe). Low impedance has low resistance, in the range of 150 to 1000 ohms (a large pipe).

A high-impedance instrument plugged into a low-impedance input is expecting to see lots of resistance to its signal flow. If the signal doesn't meet that resistance, it'll overdrive and distort the input almost immediately, no matter how low you keep the input level.

A low-impedance mic plugged into a high-impedance input meets too much resistance to its signal flow. Therefore, no matter how high you turn the input level up, there's insufficient level to obtain a proper amount of VU reading. The water from the large pipe can't all squeeze into the small pipe fast enough.

Direct Box

To match a high-impedance output to a low-impedance input or vice versa use a direct box—also called a line-matching transformer, impedance-matching transformer, impedance transformer or DI (direct injection). Its sole purpose is to change the impedance of the instrument or device plugged into its input.

Impedance transformers work equally well in both directions—low to high or high to low. Using the same transformer, you can plug a high-impedance instrument into the high-impedance input and then patch the low-impedance output into a low-impedance input, or, if necessary, you can plug low-impedance into the low-impedance end and come out of the transformer high-impedance.

Basic Terminology

- Ohm (indicated by Ω): The unit of resistance to the flow of electrical current used to measure impedance

- Impedance: Resistance to the flow of electrical current

- Z: The abbreviation and symbol used in place of the word impedance

- Hi Z: High impedance. The exact numerical tag (in Ω) for high impedance varies, depending on whether we're dealing with input impedance or output impedance. It's generally in the range of 5,000Ω to 15,000Ω for output impedance and 50,000Ω to 1,000,000Ω for input impedance. It's important here to understand that hi Z is usually greater than 5,000 to 10,000Ω.

- Lo Z: Low impedance. The exact numerical tag (in Ω) varies for low impedance as well as high impedance. It's generally in the range of 50Ω to 300Ω for output impedance. It's normal for microphone output impedance to be between 50Ω and 150Ω and 500Ω to 3,000Ω for input impedance. Normal input impedance for lo Z mixers is 600Ω. Essentially, lo Z usually uses small numbers below 600Ω.

- Output impedance: The actual impedance (resistance to the electron flow measured in Ω) at the output of a device (microphone, amplifier, guitar, keyboard). To keep it simple, realize that the output impedance is designed to work well with a specific input impedance.

- Input impedance: The actual impedance (resistance to the electron flow measured in Ω) at the input of a device. To keep it simple, realize that the input impedance is designed to work well with a specific output impedance. Low impedance and high impedance are not compatible.

Compatibility Between Hi Z and Lo Z

The reason lo and hi Z don't work together is really pretty simple. Recall our previous analogy involving a couple of simple water pipes and some water. In this analogy, water represents electricity and the size of the pipe represents the amount of impedance (Z).

Imagine a very small pipe. The small pipe represents hi Z because no matter how much water (electrical current) is at the entrance (input) of the small pipe, only a limited amount of water can get through the pipe at once. Its physical size limits the amount of water that can pass through the pipe in a period of time.

If you plug the output of a low-impedance mic into the input of a high-impedance amplifier, you have a problem. Imagine the microphone signal traveling through a very large pipe (lo Z). It's expecting to see a similar sized pipe at the input of a low-impedance amplifier. When it meets the small pipe (hi Z) at the input of the hi Z amplifier, it's impossible for the complete low-impedance signal to efficiently and accurately enter the small pipe. There's too much resistance to the signal flow; the pipe's too small.

This analogy is very appropriate because the result of plugging the output of a lo Z mic into the input of a hi Z amp is insufficient level. The amp might be turned up to maximum but you'll barely be able to hear the signal from the mic; there's too much resistance at the amplifier input.

The other incompatible scenario involves attempting to plug a high-impedance output (microphone, guitar, keyboard, etc.) into a low-impedance input (mixer, amp, speaker, etc.). In this case, the hi Z output (small pipe) is expecting to meet a hi Z input (small pipe); in other words, it's expecting to meet high resistance. If the high-impedance output signal is plugged into a low-impedance input, the signal meets practically no resistance and therefore almost immediately overdrives the input.

Practically speaking, when you plug a high-impedance guitar output into a lo Z mixer input, the input level can hardly be turned up before the VU meters read 0VU; even then, the sound you hear is

Sound Advice on Developing Your Home Studio

usually distorted because there's not
enough resistance at the input.

Hi Z Compared to Lo Z

*There's too much resistance at the hi impedance input of the amp for the low
impedance signal to accurately and efficiently enter.*

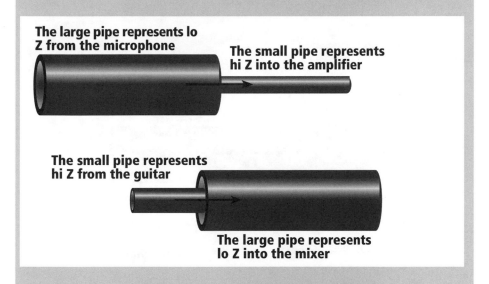

**The large pipe represents lo
Z from the microphone**

**The small pipe represents
hi Z into the amplifier**

**The small pipe represents
hi Z from the guitar**

**The large pipe represents
lo Z into the mixer**

*There's too little resistance at the low impedance input of the mixer for the
high impedance signal to accurately and efficiently enter; there's no compatibility between the output impedance of the guitar and the input impedance of
the mixer.*

Compatible Impedance

The impedances below are in accordance with the design concept: a hi Z output feeding into a hi Z input. Notice that the pipes aren't identical in size. This is part of the design and is what you'll find in real life use—both pipes are small, representing hi Z.

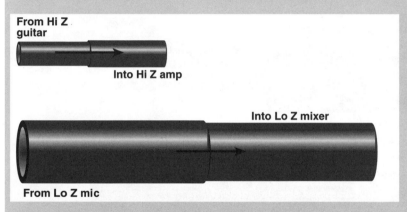

From Hi Z guitar

Into Hi Z amp

Into Lo Z mixer

From Lo Z mic

The impedances above are in accordance with the design concept: a lo Z output feeding into a lo Z input. Notice that the pipes aren't identical in size. This is part of the design and is what you will find in real life use—both pipes are large, representing lo Z.

High-impedance outputs are supposed to meet high-impedance inputs; low-impedance outputs are supposed to meet low-impedance inputs. It's not true that the input and output impedance need to be identical. In fact, the input impedance is generally supposed to be about ten times the output impedance, but as I mentioned earlier, we need to keep in mind that high impedance uses high Ω ratings (around and above 10,000Ω) and low impedance uses low Ω ratings—usually below 1,000Ω.

Line Cable

This illustration shows the construction of typical wire used for unbalanced cables. Notice that the hot lead is stranded wire in the center core; the shield is braided wire isolated from the hot lead by a plastic tube; and around the shield is a plastic or rubber insulating material.

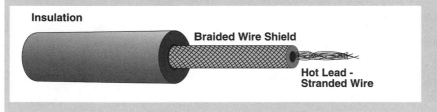

Insulation

Braided Wire Shield

Hot Lead - Stranded Wire

We can simply use an impedance transformer—also called a line matching transformer or direct box—to change impedance from high to low or low to high; that's the easy part. We should, however, strive for a thorough understanding of why we do what we do. This simple explanation of impedance is meant to get you started toward your enlightenment. It is admittedly primary in its depth, but it functions as an excellent point of reference for further technical growth.

Wiring Line Cables

This illustration shows the parts of a typical 1/4" line cable. The other common unbalanced connector is the RCA phono plug.

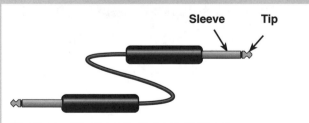

Sleeve   **Tip**

The tip carries the actual musical signal.

The sleeve is connected to the shield which is designed to absorb, diffuse and reject interference.

Balanced vs. Unbalanced

For the purposes of this course, we'll cover this topic—much like we did with impedance—using simple visual references and nontechnical language. Some of the basic differences between balanced and unbalanced wiring schemes are simple, and some of the technical differences are brilliant; let's look at these two types of wiring.

As a point of reference remember this: Almost all guitars are unbalanced and almost all low-impedance mics are balanced. If we dissect the cables that connect the guitar to the amp or the mic to the mixer, we'll learn a lot about the concept of balanced and unbalanced wiring.

Basic Terminology

- Lead: Another term for wire

- Hot lead: In a cable, the wire carrying the desired sound or signal. From a guitar, the hot lead carries the guitar signal from the magnetic pickup on the guitar to the input of the amplifier.

- Braided shield: Cables for instruments, mics and outboard gear—pretty much anything other than speaker cable— have one or two wires, or hot leads, carrying the desired signal. Surrounding the hot leads are very thin strands of wire braided into a tube so that electrostatic noises and interferences can be diffused, absorbed and rejected. This braided tube that surrounds the hot leads is called the shield.

Unbalanced Guitar Cables

Normal guitar and keyboard cables, also called line cables, contain one hot lead to carry the instrument signal. That hot lead is surrounded by a braided wire shield. The purpose of the shield is to diffuse, absorb and reject electrostatic noises and interference.

This system works pretty well within its limitations. Radio signals and other interference is kept from reaching the hot lead by the braided shield—as long as the cable is shorter than about 20 feet. Once the cable is longer than 20 feet, there's so much interference bombarding the shield that the hot lead starts to carry the interference along with the musical signal. The long cable is acting as a crude antenna and is picking up plenty of transmissions from multiple transmitters. This fact is true even when we study balanced cables; the main difference is that the balanced wiring scheme cleverly beats the system by using the system.

Balanced Cables

Almost all low-impedance mics, as well as some outboard equipment and mixers, use balanced cables. Whereas the length limit of the unbalanced cables is about 25 feet—depending on the position of the moon and the stars—balanced low-impedance cables can be as long as you need (up to

1,000 feet or so) without the addition of noise or electrostatic interference and without significant degradation of the audio signal. Pretty cool, huh?!

Wire for Balanced Cables

Most wire for balanced cables has three separate leads twisted together in the center core throughout the length of the cable. Two of the leads carry the signal and the third connects to ground via the braided shield. Sometimes there are only two center wires, in which case they are both hot; the sleeve is connected to ground via the braided shield.

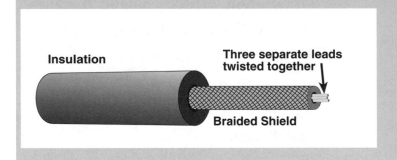

If two waveforms are 180° out of phase, they'll electronically cancel each other. It's also true that if two waveforms are exactly in phase, they'll sum, doubling in amplitude. These two theories

Sound Advice on Developing Your Home Studio

play key roles in the design of the balanced system.

A cable for a balanced lo Z mic uses three conductors, unlike the unbalanced system that just uses the hot lead and the braided shield. Of these three conductors, two are used as hot leads and the other is connected to ground. Two conductor shielded cables are also very common; the two conductors are the hot leads and the shield is connected to ground.

This is the good part and I'll explain it to you in the simplest illustrative form that I've found. The exact same signal is carried by both hot leads. The only difference is that one lead is carrying a signal from the mic that's 180° out of phase with the other lead. This is very significant; knowing this fact is crucial to the understanding of balanced wiring.

If, at any time, you were to cut the cable and combine those two hot leads, you'd hear absolutely no musical signal from the source, since the two hot leads are out of phase; the two sound waves would totally cancel each other. What you would hear would be any noise or electrostatic interference that had been absorbed up to that point. In fact, that noise would be doubled in amplitude from its normal level since both hot leads contain the same interference—completely in phase. The hot leads are twisted evenly throughout the length of the cable intentionally so that they're both subjected to the exact same interference.

Any three-point connector can be used on balanced cables. As long as there's a place for the two hot leads and a ground to connect, the system will work. XLR connectors are the most common connector, but a plug like a 1/4" phone stereo headphone plug with a tip-ring-sleeve configuration is also common. In the larger studios, a smaller version of the stereo

Sound Advice on Developing Your Home Studio

phone plug is common: the Tiny
Telephone [TT] connector.

Three-point Connectors

Any three point connector can be used on balanced cables. As long as there's a place for the two hot leads and a ground to connect, the system will work. XLR connectors are the most common, but the quarter inch tip-ring-sleeve plug—like the kind on your stereo headphones—is also common. In commercial studios, a smaller version of the quarter inch stereo plug, called the Tiny Telephone connector, is also common.

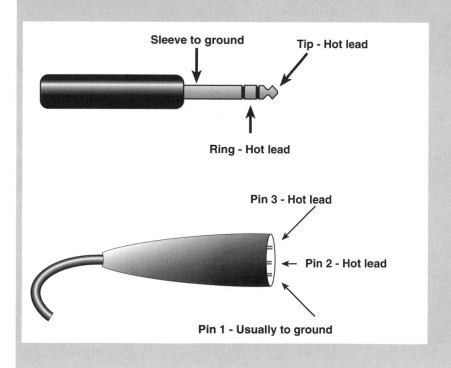

Balanced Theory

If the cable were cut anywhere between the connectors, and the hot leads were combined, we'd hear no musical signal; we would hear all noise. This is because the hot leads are 180° out of phase coming from the microphone.

Pin 3 hot is inverted phase (ø) at the mic. At the mixer, this lead is phase inverted again in order to put the musical signal back in phase with the other hot lead. At the same time this puts the noise 180° out of phase with the noise in the other hot lead therefore cancelling any noise picked up throughout the length of the cable.

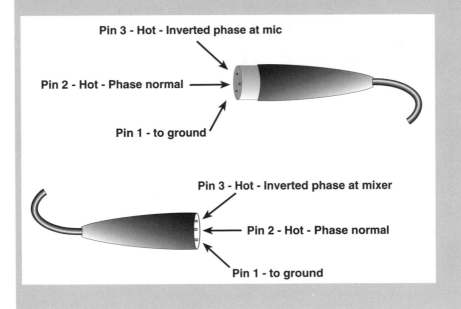

Pin 3 - Hot - Inverted phase at mic

Pin 2 - Hot - Phase normal

Pin 1 - to ground

Pin 3 - Hot - Inverted phase at mixer

Pin 2 - Hot - Phase normal

Pin 1 - to ground

Now let's look at the concept of balanced wiring that lets us use cables of up to 1,000 feet in length with no significant signal loss and no interference.

I already mentioned that at the microphone end of the cable the two hot leads are carrying the signal 180° out of phase so that if the two hot leads were combined anywhere along the cable length we wouldn't hear any of the desired musical signal. We would, however, hear lots of noise and electrostatic interference.

The completion of the system happens when, at the mixer end of the cable, the phase of one of the hot leads is inverted so that the hot leads are back in phase. Now when they're combined, the signal can be heard, plus there's a doubling in amplitude; this is good.

So, what's the benefit of inverting the phase again at the mixer end of the cable, aside from the fact that the hot leads are back in phase?

Since the noise and interference were absorbed throughout the entire length of the cable—no matter how long the cable—and since the noise is absorbed equally and is in phase on both hot leads, a most interesting thing happens when the phase of one of the hot leads is inverted at the mixer end of the cable. Any noise or interference that was picked up by the cable is totally canceled because one of the hot leads contains noise that's made to be 180° out of phase with the noise in the other hot lead. I love that part!

In summary, the result of balanced wiring is total cancellation of noise and interference, plus a doubling in amplitude compared to the signal in an unbalanced system.

Line Level

Line in and line out are common terms typically associated with tape recorder inputs and outputs and mixer inputs and outputs. The signal that comes from a microphone has a strength that's called mic level, and a mixer needs to have that signal amplified to what is called line level. The amplifier that brings the mic level up to line level is called the mic preamp.

Instrument inputs on mixers are line level. An input that is line level enters the board after the microphone preamp and is, therefore, not affected by its adjustment.

Some mixers have attenuators on the line inputs and the mic inputs to compensate for different instrument and tape recorder output levels. As we optimize each instrument or voice recording, we must optimize the gain structure at each point of the signal path. When all the levels are correct for each mic preamp, line attenuator, fader, EQ, bus fader, etc., we can record the cleanest, most accurate signal. When one link of this chain is weak, the overall sonic integrity crashes and burns.

Mixers that have only one 1/4-inch phone input on each channel typically have a Mic/Line switch. Select the appropriate position for your situation. In mic position the input goes through the preamp. In line position (possibly called instrument position) the preamp is not included.

+4dBm vs. -10dBV

You might have heard the terms plus four or minus 10 (+4 or -10) used when referring to a mixer, tape recorder or signal processor.

This is another consideration for compatibility between pieces of equipment, aside from the low impedance/high impedance dilemma. Different equipment can have different relative line level strength. This is tagged in dB and the two options are +4dBm or -10dBV.

When we use the term dB it's useful to keep in mind that it is a term that expresses a ratio between two powers and can be tagged to many different types of power that we encounter in recording.

With our option of +4dBm, dB is being tagged to milliwatts; and with -10dBV, dB is being tagged to volts. Without going into the math of it all, let's simply remember that +4 equipment only works well with other +4 equipment, and -10 equipment only works well with other -10 equipment.

Some units let you switch between +4 and -10, so all you do is select the level that matches your system. There are also boxes made that let you go in at one level and out at the other.

The Preamp

One of the first things your signal from the mic sees as it enters the mixer is the mic preamp (sometimes called the input preamp or simply the preamp). The pre-amp is actually a small amplifier circuit, and its controls are generally at the top of each channel. The preamp level controls how much a source is amplified and is sometimes labeled as the Mic Gain Trim, Mic Preamp, Input Preamp, Trim, Preamp or Gain.

Many boards have an LED (light-emitting diode, or red light) next to the preamp control. This is a peak level indicator and is used to indicate peak signal strength that either is or is getting close to overdriving the input. The proper way to adjust the preamp control is to turn it up until the peak LED is blinking occasionally, then decrease the preamp level slightly. It's usually okay if the peak LED blinks a few times during a recording.

Attenuator

Sometimes the signal that comes from a microphone or instrument into the board is too strong for the preamp stage of your mixer. This can happen when miking a very loud instrument, like a drum or electric guitar amp, or when accepting the DI of a guitar or bass with particularly powerful pickups. Some microphones can also produce a stronger signal than others. If the signal is too strong going into the preamp, then there will be unacceptable distortion.

This situation requires the use of an attenuator, also called a pad. This is almost always found at the top of each channel by the preamp level control. An attenuator restricts the flow of signal into the preamp by a measured amount or, in some cases, by a variable amount. Listen to Audio Example 8 to hear the sound of an overdriven input. This example would sound clean and clear if only the attenuator switch were set correctly!

The Overdriven Input

Most attenuators include 10, 20 or 30dB pads, which are labeled -10dB, -20dB, or -30dB.

If there's noticeable distortion from a sound source, even if the preamp is turned down, use the pad. Start with the least amount of pad available first. If distortion disappears, all is well. If there's still distortion, try more attenuation.

Once the distortion is gone, use the preamp level control to attain sufficient input level. Listen to Audio Example 9 to hear the dramatic difference this adjustment can make in the clarity of an audio signal.

Audio Example 9
Attenuator Adjustment

Input Level Comparison

These initial variables are very important points for us to deal with. Any good engineer has a solid grasp of these crucial parts of the signal path. These are the basics; you'll continually return to them for clean, quality, professional recordings.

Listen to Audio Examples 10, 11 and 12. If your signal isn't clean and accurate at the input stage, it won't be clean and accurate anywhere.

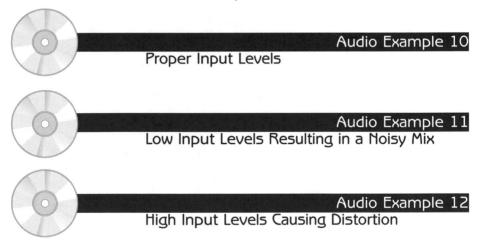

Audio Example 10
Proper Input Levels

Audio Example 11
Low Input Levels Resulting in a Noisy Mix

Audio Example 12
High Input Levels Causing Distortion

Patch Bays

One tool that's essential to any setup is a patch bay—nothing more than a panel with jacks in the front and jacks on the back. Jack #1 on the front is connected to Jack #1 on the back, #2 on the front to #2 on the back and so on.

If all available ins and outs for all of your equipment are patched into the back of a patch bay and the corresponding points in the front of the patch bay are clearly labeled, you'll never need to search laboriously behind equipment again just to connect two pieces of gear together. All patching can be done with short, easy-to-patch cables on the front of the patch bay.

Patch bays are used for line level patches like channel ins and outs, tape recorder line ins and outs, sound module outputs and any signal processor ins and outs. Don't use the patch bay for powered outputs, like the speaker outputs of your power amplifiers.

Sound Advice on Developing Your Home Studio

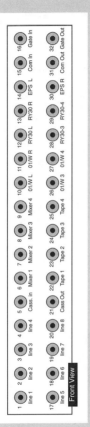

If all available ins and outs of your equipment are patched into the back of a patch bay, and if the corresponding points in the front of the patch bay are clearly labeled, your sessions will be more efficient. You'll free yourself from searching behind equipment in all sorts of contorted positions, just to connect two pieces of gear together. All patching can be done with short, easy-to-patch cables on the front of the patch bay. Patch bays are made using most standard types of jacks:

- RCA patch bays are the least expensive and work very well in a home recording situation.
- TT (tiny telephone) patch bays use a small tip-ring-sleeve connector.
- 1/4" phone patch bays are very solid and are the most dependable for ultimate plug-to-jack contact.

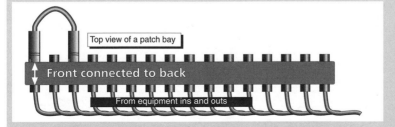

Top view of a patch bay

Front connected to back

From equipment ins and outs

Patch Bay with Easy Patches

*Patch bays are used for line level patches like channel ins and outs, tape recorder line ins and outs, sound module outputs and any signal processor ins and outs. **Don't use the patch bay for powered outputs, like the speaker outputs from your power amplifiers.** Patch bays are for line level signals. Only in very special cases will patch bays carry mic level signals, but they almost never contain powered signals.*

If all the line ins to each channel on your mixer are connected to the back of a patch bay and all the outputs of all of your synthesizers and sound modules are connected to the back of the same patch bay, the task of patching any keyboard into any channel becomes very simple, fast and efficient.

If all channel inserts, sends and returns are patched to a patch bay, it becomes simple and fast to patch an EQ, compressor, gate or any other piece of signal processing into any channel.

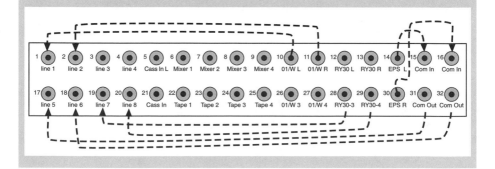

The concept of easy and efficient patching becomes obvious when it's explained, and once you've made the move to include a patch bay in your setup, you'll never go back, because you'll be able to accomplish more, faster and more efficiently.

Acoustic Considerations

No matter what high-tech gear you've combined with classic vintage gear, if certain acoustic considerations haven't been addressed, you're going to have a rough time getting world class sounds. Vocals recorded in an empty bedroom are brutally damaged by standing waves and unwanted reflections. Once they're on tape or disc, they can't be made to sound as smooth and warm as they could have if they'd been recorded in a properly treated acoustic environment.

Somehow, your studio must be broken up acoustically. At home, most of us operate in a bedroom-sized recording room that acts as a studio, control room, machine room, storage room, maintenance room, office, and possibly bedroom. The disadvantage to this setup is that you can't spread out into areas that are optimized for a specific purpose. The advantage is that you probably have a lot of stuff in your studio—stuff that absorbs, reflects, and diffuses sound waves.

Though you might have a lot of furniture and gear in your studio, additional help should be considered. Shaping the space around your recording microphones is clearly advantageous, especially in a room that is acoustically live. Live acoustics are good when they're been designed to enhance the acoustic properties of a voice or an instrument. When acoustics are randomly active, they are potentially destructive and must be controlled.

Physical structures within the acoustic space provide the best confusion of otherwise detrimental waves. Though soft surfaces dampen high frequencies, the low-mids, which can be most damaging to sound, must be diffused or reflected in order to insure a smooth, even frequency response. Listen to Audio Examples 13 and 14. The first version demonstrates the intense room sound on a vocal mic in my family room. The second version demonstrates the same setup with the addition of a tool called a Studio Trap, from Acoustic Sciences Corporation.

Audio Example 13
Voice With and Without Studio Traps

When absorption panels are hung on the studio walls and tools like the Tube Trap or baffles are used to confuse standing waves, the sounds you record are easier to mix. All of a sudden, your recordings sound more like the hits you hear on professional recordings. To overlook these considerations is to create a troublesome situation for your recording and mixing

Molding the Recording Environment

Using a device like the Studio Trap from Acoustic Sciences Corp. (ASC) can make the difference between an amateur sound and a world class sound. Whether at home or in a commercial studio, we must always be aware of how the acoustical environment affects recorded sound quality.

In the example below, the vocalist and microphone are surrounded by the Studio Traps in a way that creates just the right acoustical feel. Using moveable devices provides the engineer the opportunity to customize each recording scenario by repositioning the Traps to support the sonic requirements of the music.

sessions. Whether tracking or mixing, address these issues so your music can have the best possible chance of impacting the listener with the power and emotion you know it deserves.

Audio Examples 14 and 15 demonstrate more settings that benefit from acoustical treatment.

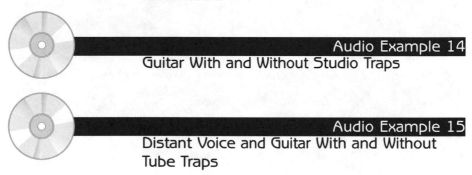

Audio Example 14
Guitar With and Without Studio Traps

Audio Example 15
Distant Voice and Guitar With and Without Tube Traps

Chips or Tubes

Though solid-state technology was originally appealing because of its lightweight and efficient power delivery, it lacked the warmth and emotional appeal of tube technology. The distortion sound created by an overdriven transistor is not appealing.

Solid-state Clipping versus Tube Distortion

Waveform A represents Waveforms B and C before they were electronically distorted.

Solid-state distortion (Waveform B) has a harsh and irritating sound. Signals that surpass maximum electronic amplitude limits are simply cut off (clipped).

Tube distortion reacts in a more gently attenuated, rounded off fashion (Waveform B). The waveforms aren't clipped. They're acted on more like an extreme limiting effect. Even though the waveform is still distorted, the resulting sound is warmer, smoother and less irritating than solid-state distortion.

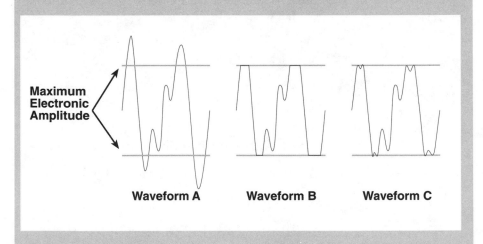

Maximum Electronic Amplitude

Waveform A　　**Waveform B**　　**Waveform C**

It's harsh, brittle sounding, and grates on one's nerves. For this reason, the tube amplifier never died; in fact, it flourished as more and more guitarists, in particular, saw the light. Tubes sound better than transistors when they are overdriven—and what guitarist do you know who doesn't overdrive their setup?

The same thing happened in the microphone and mic preamp arena. Engineers all over started realizing that the vintage tube mics, preamps, and compressors built in the '50s and '60s sounded warmer and smoother than the newer technology of solid-state equipment.

Both tube and solid-state equipment have a viable place in recording and can peacefully coexist to the musician's benefit. I've found that whenever I need a pristine sound, I use a clean solid-state device that has lots of headroom. Some of the cleanest, clearest, and most accurate sounds come from solid-state condenser microphones through excellent solid-state preamps. These devices are amazingly clean and accurate up to the point where their circuitry is overdriven in even the slightest amount. Once they reach the point of distortion, everything quickly falls to pieces and the sound they produce is undesirable. Who knows, though? Maybe someday you'll use that sound in a way that revolutionizes the audio industry.

When you want a sound that is aggressive and even the slightest bit overdriven, try a tube mic through a tube preamp. As the tube circuitry begins to distort, it rounds off the peaks of the waveforms. In contrast, solid-state circuits clip the tops off the waveforms. The sound of the tube circuits distorting is much smoother and warmer than the sound of the solid-state circuitry distorting.

Listen to Audio Example 16. Notice the difference in the sound of the vocal as

Sound Advice on Developing Your Home Studio

the signal path switches from solid-state to tube.

Vocal on a Tube then Solid-state Mic

Now listen to Audio Examples 17. Notice the difference in the sound of the acoustic guitar as I switch from a tube setup to a solid-state setup.

Guitar on a Tube then Solid-state Condenser Microphoner

Each microphone manufacturer, each model, and each individual microphone have a unique personality. Variations between specific mics, even of the same model, are sometimes extreme. In a studio with ten U87s, it doesn't take long to find the one or two units that stand out as the best sounding of the bunch. With this is mind, it's not always fair to say one type of mic or preamp is any better than another.

It all comes down to the specific mic choice, the specific instrument, and the specific piece of music. Listen to the differences in the recorded vocal sound from the tube microphones. They're all good mics, but each has a different sonic character and would be a great choice for some applications and a poor choice for others. Even identical models from one manufacturer might sound substantially different. Assess each mic on its own sonic merit.

Combining Tubes and Chips

Many great sounds are achieved through the combined use of tube and solid-state technology. It's common to use a tube microphone in conjunction with a solid-state preamp or a solid-state mic along with a tube preamp. This technique takes advantage of the warmth and depth of the tube sound, yet keeps the amount of tube sound in check through the use of ultra clean solid-state circuitry throughout the remainder of the signal path. For this very

Sound Advice on Developing Your Home Studio

reason, several devices are available that include both tube and solid-state signal paths.

With the continuing controversy over the merits of tube equipment compared to solid-state gear, it's the engineer's responsibility to know the sonic character of each tool available. If you know the personality of the tools at hand, you'll be better equipped to augment your setup with additional gear. Your choices will be informed, educated, and respected.

Preamps

Microphone preamps are as different as microphones. To say that you love the sound of tube preamps is a bit dangerous. To say that solid-state preamps sound harsh and brittle isn't a secure platform on which to stand. There are some incredibly smooth and warm-sounding tube preamps; and there are others that are not so smooth and warm. There are some harsh sounding solid-state preamps, but there are many wonderful sounding solid-state preamps. Many solid-state units exude purity, smoothness, and pristine clarity.

Old Effects versus New

The audio industry is very driven by advertising. Once the new multi-effects processor hits the street, we lose respect for the old. But look at your effects as tools. Nothing sounds just like an old Yamaha Rev 7. It might not be the cleanest or the easiest to use by today's standards, but it has a personality that's unique and applicable to many situations. The Lexicon Prime Time digital delay was one of the first digital devices, and it still sounds good blended into the lead vocal track. If you're fortunate enough to have some real Master Room spring reverb cylinders around or an old AMS plate reverb, consider yourself blessed. These tools have amazing personality. Keep all your Quadraverbs, MIDIVerbs, Reflexes, etc. If you're not using them a lot, at least wire them into a patch bay and remember they're available. Using these powerful tools combined with the new and amazing technological breakthroughs helps add individuality and character to your music.

Mixers

In the upper echelon of audio recording, many engineers and producers prefer the sound of vintage large format consoles. Neve and Solid State Logic consoles dominate the upper-end studios. Neve is known for its smooth, clean sound. Solid State Logic is known for its aggressive edge. Having worked on both, I can attest to the fact that they are what they're assumed to be and that they each have a personality that matches their reputation. The problem is that they're amazingly expensive. In addition, when I mix on a huge Neve VR series console with Flying Faders, I feel limited in what I can accomplish. The automation is archaic in comparison to the new digital consoles that serious home recordists can justify buying. The sound is very good, but the sound is also good on many of the new digital mixers. The Mackie D8B has amazing headroom in its preamps and includes Apogee converters. The sound quality is incredible. The Yamaha 02/R has been used for many very successful and wonderful sounding projects. Even the smaller and very affordable digital mixers offer good sound quality and tons of features.

Whereas the recording studio of the past centered around one huge console with an operator, the recording studio of the future will center more and more around a creative individual who can make incredible music.